A Conceptual Prototype for the Next-Generation National Elevation Dataset

By Jason M. Stoker, Hans Karl Heidemann, Gayla A. Evans, and Susan K. Greenlee

Open-File Report 2013-1023

U.S. Department of the Interior
U.S. Geological Survey

U.S. Department of the Interior
KEN SALAZAR, Secretary

U.S. Geological Survey
Marcia K. McNutt, Director

U.S. Geological Survey, Reston, Virginia: 2013

For more information on the USGS—the Federal source for science about the Earth,
its natural and living resources, natural hazards, and the environment—visit
http://www.usgs.gov or call 1–888–ASK–USGS

For an overview of USGS information products, including maps, imagery, and publications,
visit *http://www.usgs.gov/pubprod*
To order this and other USGS information products, visit *http://store.usgs.gov*

Suggested citation:

Stoker, J.M., Heidemann, Hans Karl, Evans, G.A., and Greenlee, S.K, 2013, A conceptual prototype for the next-generation national elevation dataset: U.S. Geologial Survey Open-File Report 2013-1023, 52 p.

Any use of trade, firm, or product names is for descriptive purposes only and does not imply
endorsement by the U.S. Government.

Contents

Figures

Tables

A Conceptual Prototype for the Next-Generation National Elevation Dataset

By Jason Stoker, Hans K. Heidemann, Gayla Evans and Susan Greenlee

Abstract

In 2012 the U.S. Geological Survey's (USGS) National Geospatial Program (NGP) funded a study to develop a conceptual prototype for a new National Elevation Dataset (NED) design with expanded capabilities to generate and deliver a suite of bare earth and above ground feature information over the United States. This report details the research on identifying operational requirements based on prior research, evaluation of what is needed for the USGS to meet these requirements, and development of a possible conceptual framework that could potentially deliver the kinds of information that are needed to support NGP's partners and constituents. This report provides an initial proof-of-concept demonstration using an existing dataset, and recommendations for the future, to inform NGP's ongoing and future elevation program planning and management decisions. The demonstration shows that this type of functional process can robustly create derivatives from lidar point cloud data; however, more research needs to be done to see how well it extends to multiple datasets.

Introduction

In the past decade, the elevation user community has become increasingly sophisticated and requires a wider range of information products than what is currently (2012) offered by the National Elevation Dataset (NED). The NED needs to be modernized to meet the National Geospatial Program

(NGP) Communities of Use, which include priority applications such as water, natural resource conservation, geologic mapping, and natural hazards. The NED, which provides bare earth data originally derived from U.S. Geological Survey (USGS) topographic quadrangles, is in 2012 being primarily developed from light detection and ranging (lidar) data and interferometric synthetic aperture radar (IfSAR); however, the NED does not currently exploit the full range of products that can be extracted from these source data. As a result, the USGS NGP is not realizing the full benefits from its investment in or the capabilities of these technologies. Lidar provides a rich set of three-dimensional (3D) points, much of which is not being used when only bare earth information is provided. The purpose of this study was to explore a conceptual system to take full advantage of elevation source data and derivative products and services to meet the Nation's elevation needs. In 2012, the NGP funded a study to develop a conceptual model of what the next-generation NED might look like. This report summarizes requirements, defines deficiencies in the current processes, and offers considerations and a possible framework for the next generation NED.

What is the NED?

The NED is the primary elevation data product produced and distributed by the USGS (Gesch and others, 2002; Gesch, 2007). The NED provides seamless raster elevation data of the conterminous United States, Alaska, Hawaii, and the island territories. The NED is derived from diverse source data sets that are processed to a specification with a consistent resolution, coordinate system, elevation units, and horizontal and vertical datums. The NED is the logical result of the maturation of the long-standing USGS elevation program, which for many years concentrated on production of topographic maps that represented elevations using contours at different elevation intervals. The NED interpolated these contours to derive a consistent, machine-readable gridded elevation dataset that is now being replaced by data generated by modern lidar and IfSAR technologies. The NED serves as the elevation layer of

The National Map, and provides basic elevation information for earth science studies and mapping applications in the United States.

The NED is a multiresolution dataset that is updated bimonthly to integrate newly available, improved elevation source data. NED data are available nationally at grid spacings of 1-arc-second (about 30 meters) and 1/3-arc-second (about 10 meters), and for limited areas at 1/9-arc-second (about 3 meters). Most of the NED data for Alaska are available at 2-arc-second (about 60 meters) grid spacing, where only lower resolution source data exist. A portion of Alaska is available at the 1/3-arc-second resolution, and plans are in development for a substantial upgrade in elevation data coverage of the State for the next 5 years. Specifications for the NED include the following:

- Coordinate system: Geographic (decimal degrees of latitude and longitude)

- Horizontal datum: North American Datum of 1983 (NAD 83)

- Vertical datum: North American Vertical Datum of 1988 (NAVD 88)

- Elevation units: Decimal meters

A good elevation source is the number one requirement for Earth science applications. In 2012, the NED is the authoritative source of public access elevation data. Scientists and resource managers use NED data for global change research, hydrologic modeling, resource monitoring, mapping and visualization, and many other applications. The NED is used in the academic world by professors and students as an educational tool and free resource for project-based studies. The NED is also the base layer of the USTopo contour generation activities.

This approach fits well with the concept, in which the best available data are easily accessible to all and unrestricted sharing of quality spatial data among users facilitates a wide range of applications.

The NED source data come from various production methods and the data can be supplied in various formats with various projections, resolution, and units. During NED preparations, data are merged into a science-ready standard dataset where anomalies and edge-matching issues have been resolved. This process enables scientists to quickly proceed with their research rather than spending time stitching together maps as was the process before NED. The NED also eliminates duplication of effort by highly skilled scientists.

The bimonthly updates of the NED provide a means of constantly improving the NED multiresolution data layers and providing the best available data to the public. The addition of lidar to the NED has resulted in updated data, enabled a new 1/9-arc-second layer to be generated, and improved vertical and horizontal accuracy of the lower resolution layers, which are derived from the improved data (fig. 1).

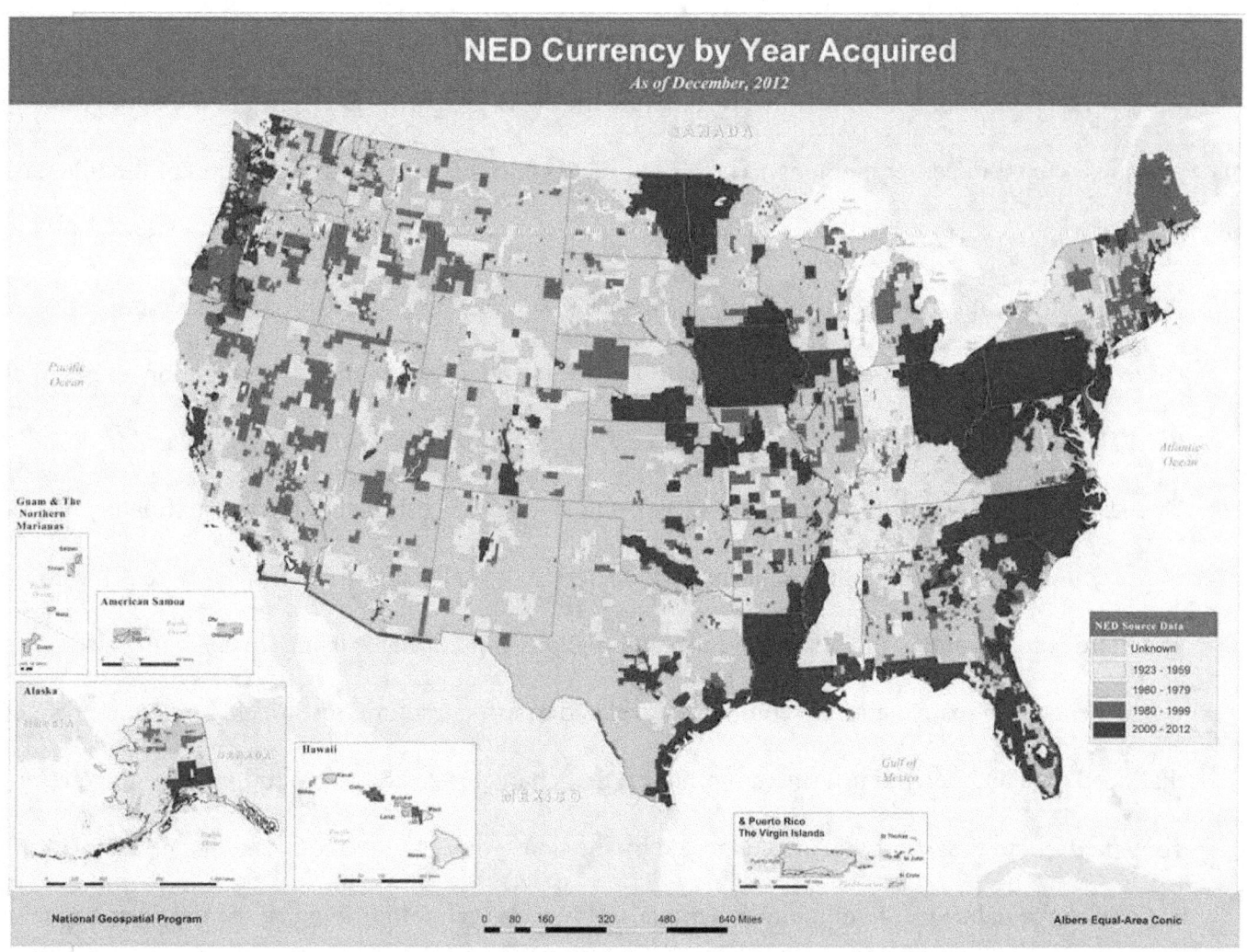

Figure 1. Example of National Elevation Dataset temporal information.

The NED data are available in three delivery methods: clip and ship, tile download, and bulk data delivery. The clip and ship method allows the customer to specify an area of interest and immediately download the data. Tile download allows a customer to select prepackaged tiles that have been zipped for download. The bulk data delivery provides the whole NED layer of a specific resolution on a physical hard drive. All of these methods include spatial and textual metadata.

Why Change the NED Now?

The lidar data being collected to generate the NED provide 3-D information that did not previously exist in earlier methods. The NED process currently uses only a fraction of the lidar source data content in producing the bare-earth models and does not provide other derivative products leaving the other information to be extracted by other means, such as simply downloading the source point cloud data from another entity (that is, USGS Center for lidar Information Coordination and Knowledge (CLICK)(*http://lidar.cr.usgs.gov*), Digital Coast (*http://www.csc.noaa.gov/digitalcoast/*), Opentopography (*http://opentopography.org*), and so on). It is estimated that approximately 30 percent of the conterminous United States has been collected by lidar for disparate projects across the country, and there is a movement to collect the entire continental United States using this technology.

There are many national requirements related to infrastructure, resources, forestry, and so on, that need data and derived information products that characterize above ground features that are not contained in the NED, but that are supported by the lidar point cloud. Requirements, new tools for exploiting the data, and the ubiquitous demands of mobile technology suggest the need for a modernized NED.

The National Enhanced Elevation Assessment

The case for a modernized NED is supported by the results of the National Enhanced Elevation Assessment (NEEA) (Dewberry, 2011). The NEEA was conducted to (1) document national-level requirements for improved elevation data, (2) estimate the benefits and costs to meet those requirements, and (3) evaluate several national-level program implementation scenarios. The assessment was sponsored by the member agencies of the National Digital Elevation Program. The study participants came from 34 Federal agencies, agencies from all 50 States, selected local government and Tribal offices, and private and not-for-profit organizations. A total of 602 mission-critical activities were identified with requirements for substantially more accurate data than what are currently available. The results of the assessment indicate that an interagency national-enhanced elevation data program has the potential to generate up to $13 billion in new benefits annually (Snyder, 2012a). Benefit-cost analyses were developed for a variety of 25 program scenarios at various levels of complexity, data quality and replacement cycles, and cost (Dewberry, 2011). Each scenario would implement a national data-collection strategy to achieve cost efficiencies and meet the requirements of multiple organizations.

The NEEA also reviewed current and emerging commercial elevation-data technologies, assessed data life-cycle-management costs for the various scenarios, and produced an inventory of existing elevation data derived from lidar and IfSAR datasets.

3D Elevation Program

Based on the NEEA results, the 3D Elevation Program (3DEP) was developed by the USGS in coordination with its Federal and State partner agencies. The primary goal of 3DEP is to systematically collect enhanced elevation data in the form of high-quality lidar data over the conterminous United States, Hawaii, and the U.S. territories on an 8-year schedule. IfSAR data will be collected over Alaska, where the cloud cover and the remote location preclude the use of lidar over much of the State. It is expected that private-sector data-acquisition companies will mobilize to respond to these lidar and IfSAR data needs and that the products and services will be accessible to all levels of government and the public. 3DEP will provide easy access to these authoritative data and derived products nationally, and at higher resolution and accuracy than are available today (Snyder, 2012b).

Current State of Development

This report provides a model for modernizing the NED to meet current national requirements for elevation data. Table 1 from the NEEA report (Dewberry, 2011) provides a summary of current elevation data and capabilities compared to the data and capabilities that are needed to meet national needs. This comparison indicates that there are many opportunities for enhancing the NED, to include improved data and derived products and services that utilize the full lidar point cloud.

Table 1. What users currently have compared to what they actually need (Dewberry, 2011).

What users have	What users need
Currently, approximately 28.4 percent of the lower 49 States and Washington D.C. has lidar data, and approximately 15.2 percent of Alaska has IFSAR data; nationwide, enhanced elevation datasets are growing at a slow annual rate and some States might never be mapped	Total U.S. coverage with enhanced elevation data.
Most digital elevation models (DEMs) in the National Elevation Dataset were produced from old quad maps accurate to 5–10 feet at the 90 percent confidence level	Most business uses require DEMs accurate to 6–12 inches at the 90 percent confidence level
Most DEMs in the NED have 1/3-arc-second (10-meter) post spacing	Require high-resolution DEMs nationwide with 1/27-arc-second (1-meter) post spacing
Most DEMs in the NED were produced from quad maps 30–50 years old	Require current DEMs nationwide with update frequencies no greater than 10 years.
Hydro-flattened DEMs in the NED where bridges and culverts impede the flow of water in hydrologic models	Require hydro-flattened and hydro-enforced DEMs where bridges/culverts are "cut" so DEMs model the actual flow of water
All DEMs in the NED are gridded Digital Terrain Models (DTMs) of the bare-earth terrain	Require gridded DTMs and Digital Surface Models (DSMs) of tree tops, roof tops, towers, etc.
No contours or hillshades are provided	Both contours and hillshades are required
From USGS' Elevation Derivatives for National Applications (EDNA) program, some slope and aspect data are available from low resolution DEMs (30-meter post spacing)	Require nationwide slope and aspect data from higher resolution DEMs (3-meter or 1-meter post spacing)
Lidar point cloud data are partially provided by USGS and other agencies	Require reliable comprehensive access to lidar point cloud data that supports diverse applications analysis of above ground features including vegetation structure
Poor metadata where currency, accuracy and data production methods are often unknown	Require good metadata where currency, accuracy and data production methods are well documented
Inadequate data discovery mechanisms to know what data are available nationwide and plans for future acquisitions and partnerships	Require improved data discovery mechanisms to support increased partnering among Federal, State and local agencies.
Elevation data acquired by State and local governments are often nonstandard and cannot be entered in the NED; some datasets are proprietary and not in the NED	Require common guidelines and specifications so that data acquired by diverse Federal, State and local governments is more consistent, and is more useful for updating the NED.

Top 10 Business Uses the NED 2.0/3DEP Must Address

The NEEA study tallied the annual benefits by business use from enhanced elevation data. It is important to take these uses into account when designing NED 2.0 / 3DEP (table 2).

Table 2. Top 10 business uses identified in the National Enhanced Elevation Assessment report.

Number	Business use	Conservative benefits (millions)	Potential benefits (millions)
1	Flood Risk Management	$440	$787
2	Infrastructure and Construction Management	$246	$974
3	Natural Resources Conservation	$169	$337
4	Agriculture and Precision Farming	$122	$2,011
5	Water Supply and Quality	$85	$156
6	Wildfire Management, Planning and Response	$84	$166
7	Geologic Resource Assessment and Hazard Mitigation	$54	$1,069
8	Forest Resources Management	$43	$61
9	River and Stream Resource Management	$23	$41
10	Aviation Navigation and Safety	$35	$56

Data Requirements Identified in the NEEA Study

The NEEA study identified some key derived elevation products that are needed by a large set of users. The lidar point cloud source data are also a highly desired product, so it would appear that NED should be focusing on the most efficient way to handle, process, and deliver point cloud data and an associated suite of derived information products. A description of these products follows.

- **Digital Terrain Model (DTM) or Digital Surface Model (DSM)**

  - The DTM is a representation of a bare-earth surface that can include irregularly spaced mass points and breaklines. DSMs currently are not provided by the USGS. The first returns from lidar point cloud data yield the DSM; users can generate their own DSMs if they have standard Geographic Information Systems (GIS) software. IfSAR data also yield DSMs. DSMs could be provided to the public if the USGS has the resources to provide them.

- **Hydrologic Processing**

  - **Hydro-Enforced DEMs**

    - Not currently provided by USGS. DEMs are used for many forms of hydrographic and hydraulic modeling; hydro-enforced DEMs are more popular than the hydro-flattened DEMs produced by USGS for mapping applications. Typical hydro-enforcement can be done by users who apply their own modeling rules for hydro-enforcement. Hydro-enforcement can become expensive, especially when including all small culverts that drain water from one side of the road to the other. Flow modeling can be complex. For instance, some culverts enable water to flow in either direction. Hydro-enforced DEMs potentially could be provided to the public.

- **Hydro-Flattened DEM/DTM**

  - The hydro-flattened DEM, where all water bodies are rendered to have flat surfaces, is a standard deliverable under the USGS lidar Specification (Heidemann, 2012). Water bodies are represented as a hydro-flattened format in the NED.

  - The bare-earth points and breaklines as specified in the USGS Lidar Specification (Heidemann, 2012) comprise a DTM; although both map the bare-earth terrain, the major difference between a DEM and DTM is that the DEM has a uniform grid, but the DTM can include irregularly spaced mass points and breaklines. DEMs and limited breaklines currently are provided by the NED.

- **Contours**
    - Whereas irregularly spaced DTMs or gridded DEMs are used for computerized analyses of bare-earth terrain surfaces, contours have long been used for human visualization of terrain surfaces. It requires time and expense to make the contours aesthetically pleasing, especially for treatment of roads and drainage features. With standard GIS software, users can generate their own contour lines, but they are normally noisy and not aesthetically pleasing. The recommended alternative is to depict terrain using a hill-shading effect, which is relatively easy to create.

- **Hillshades**
    - Not currently provided by the USGS. Users with their own GIS software can generate their own hill-shading. This is an appropriate application for commercial development for use on personal computers and mobile devices such as smart phones.

- **Slope**
    - The USGS no longer provides slope data from EDNA (Elevation Derivatives for National Applications) for 1-arc-second data only. Users with their own GIS software can generate their own slope maps using higher-resolution DEMs or point cloud data.

- **Aspect**
    - The USGS no longer provides aspect data from EDNA for 1-arc-second data only. Users with their own GIS software can generate their own aspect maps using higher-resolution DEMs or point cloud data.

- **Curvature**

- The USGS currently does not provide curvature data from Elevation Derivatives for National Applications (EDNA). Instead, curvature data are user-generated using standard GIS software.

Data Requirements Not Identified in the Study but Deemed Important to Meet Business Use Requirements

The NEEA study primarily reached a community of use that was already familiar with elevation data. It is expected, however, there is a substantial number of organizations that may not be familiar with the utility of elevation data to support their business needs. The NED 2.0 should support NEEA-identified needs as well as other newly emerging and anticipated needs. With this in mind, some supplemental derivatives, that are reasonably easy to extract from a lidar point cloud, may also prove valuable in applications such as the following:

- **Height Above Ground**
  - This is simply a raster calculation where the DTM elevation is subtracted from the DSM elevation. The derived resolution is a function of the pixel size of the DTM and DSM data. This calculation provides the height of features above the ground. Tree/canopy heights and building footprints/heights can easily be extracted from this derivative.

- **Laser Intensity**
  - Simply put, this is the strength of the signal reflection from the target(s) back to the lidar instrument, normalized by pulse energy out. Reflectance can be viewed as a panchromatic image where each pixel value is an indication of how strongly a laser pulse is reflected off the target. Intensity images are useful because they are inherently georeferenced, which allows for photogrammetric-like stereo compilation of breaklines and other features. Currently there is no standardized method for calibrating or normalizing an intensity image, which means the same

type of object may reflect at a different intensity based on a wide range of factors (that is, flying height, beam divergence, scan angle, etc.); however, the compilation of images from intensity values in the point cloud is relatively straightforward.

- **Number of Returns/Density**

  - A raster-based count of number of returned laser signals and their order per emitted pulse, within a pixel area, could be a useful product. This measure could be used for checking the density of data on a per-pixel basis, or for classifying the pixels. For example if USGS NGP-collected data require a minimum of 1 point per 2 meter cell, and allow for no data voids except over water, raster images can be generated to show how many points there are in each 2 meter cell as a measure of data quality. Also, pixels with intermediate returns generally indicate the presence of vegetation, so that a vegetation mask can be generated using this raster image.

- **Enhanced Spatial Metadata**

  - As most airborne lidar datasets are collected and organized by flight line (also called a 'lift'), the new NED metadata should begin documenting spatial data by project and by flight line. As a result, the project metadata records and preserves information for the entire collection and is a good summary of the project. Providing metadata per flight line would be valuable because errors in the data could be identified and corrected more easily, thus giving the consumer a better idea of the nature of the data and how it behaved in the collection.

  - Ensure metadata includes the geoid model used to convert ellipsoid heights to orthometric heights, if used. Then, when the new vertical datum is adopted, reprocess all existing orthometric heights to reflect the new geoid heights.

- **Change Source Data and Information Product's Projection, Resolution and File Type**

- Whereas this is more of a service than a derivative, being able to change attributes of the data to better meet individual's needs could allow for more uses of the data. If a user can reproject the data before generating derived products, the accuracy of those products will be improved.

  - There is a strong desire by the user community for 1-meter resolution derivatives for local applications. Although the source data may be able to support those resolutions, it is simply not practical to store the entire United States at a pre-computed 1-meter resolution. It is computationally inefficient in terms of storage and time; therefore, the ability to create the 1/27th arc-second derived products by a customizable derivative generator would only be located in areas where there is demand for such a product.

Requirements Identified as Important but Impractical for NED 2.0/3DEP

- **Triangulated Irregular Networks (TINS)**
  - Although TINs often are used to create other products (for example, gridded DEMs, contours, slope maps), it is not realistic for TINs to be provided to the public because TIN triangles cross tile boundaries and are not easily tiled for distribution, and because TINs have much larger file sizes, carrying the topological data structure of each individual TIN triangle relative to adjoining triangles. TINs can best be produced by users with their own GIS software.

- **Breaklines**
  - The USGS collects breaklines only as required for hydro-flattening. Breaklines can be expensive to compile, but there is a decreased need for breaklines as there is an increase in lidar point density. Because there are many different types of breaklines, this task is best left to

individual users who best know their requirements for breaklines and best know what they can afford.

- **Cross Sections**

  - The USGS does not provide cross sections and it is unrealistic for the agency to do so in the future because there are an infinite number of possible cross sections that could be drawn within each cell of lidar data. Users with GIS software can generate their own cross sections to meet their unique needs. There is, however, an opportunity to provide a cross-section service by the web that allows users to generate their own cross sections.

New Capabilities the NED 2.0 / 3DEP Needs to Have to Best Meet Business Use Requirements

Preparing the new NED to be able to incorporate a potential 3D Elevation Program is paramount to its survival. By developing NED 2.0 before this program is in the development phase, NED will be setting the stage for how this program should develop. The NEEA report details several important points that NED 2.0 / 3DEP need to consider in its development, which may change the workflow considerably. A basic workflow as defined in the NEEA report (Dewberry, 2011) is shown in figure2.

Figure 2. Basic workflow identified in the National Enhanced Elevation Assessment report.

- **Data Provisioning**—The source data that become part of the national enhanced elevation product will need to be made available to users for query and download. In general, web technology is used to allow these users to determine the data that are available and request downloads for subset areas of the data. Some provisioning of larger datasets may be required through removable disk media. Additional functionality may be available to the user from the web, including more robust queries (for example, determine the elevation of a point or line), viewing the data products in a web browser map, integrating the data into other web or desktop mapping products with web services, and doing user customized processing of the data to create new data products. In general, this task will be automated, with little manual labor involved.

- **Data Investigation**—Web- and file-based data investigations will be the primary mechanisms for the next few years; however, with the advent of the cloud, commercial off the shelf (COTS) programs could 'talk to' the NED 2.0/3DEP database, allowing users to access directly NED 2.0/3DEP data in their own software. ArcGIS is moving forward on this type of technology, and the software package Global Mapper has some capability to use online geospatial data. In order for this to happen, either the data must reside outside the USGS firewall, or there must be a mechanism for the software to know what data are behind the firewall and access them accordingly. Putting data in a cloud environment may be an option as well, and should be a topic of active research.

- **Data Storage**—Data received from source providers need to be made available to quality control technicians for review. As source data are received and are ready for quality control, the data will need to be placed in storage accessible from software used for data reviews. The initial review will be followed by data processing, which will require storage of the source and output data files.

- **Archival**—Data need to be archived for long-term preservation and for historical reference. Data that are archived may include the original source data received from source providers, as well as the finalized and accepted national elevation data products. These data should be archived in a manner that ensures their preservation under extreme circumstances, including disasters or system failure. Best practices often require copies to be stored offline in two geographically distinct locations, with the primary location easily accessible and a secondary location in a more secure environment.

- **Data Download**—Similar to data investigation, users should be able to download data by a web portal, a file location system, or through software that can access part or the entire NED 2.0/3DEP database, either by the cloud or through a firewall. Improving download experiences should be a topic of active research.

Technology Trends and Risk Considerations

In the NEEA study, Dewberry (2011) evaluated the opportunities, challenges, and risks to a nationwide enhanced elevation program. It is prudent to keep these factors in mind moving forward with NED 2:

- Changes to topographic lidar technologies.

- Changes to bathymetric and topobathymetric lidar technologies.

- Evolving airborne and satellite IFSAR technologies, including the changing role of satellite Differential Interferometric Synthetic Aperture Radar (DINSAR) for repeat-pass interferometry.

- Changes to enabling technologies, including inertial measurement units (IMUs), airborne GPS, and Continuously Operating Reference Stations (CORS).

- Changes to the geoid model resulting from National Geodetic Survey (NGS) Gravity for the Redefinition of the American Vertical Datum (GRAV-D) project.

- NGS changes to the horizontal and vertical datums in the 2020s from which all geospatial coordinates are referenced.

- Capacity of commercial lidar vendors to collect and process data in a timely and cost-effective manner.

- Evolving lidar standards and guidelines.

- Evolving lidar quality assurance/quality control (QA/QC) procedures.

- Uncertainties in the ability of the USGS to deliver standard elevation products, elevation derivatives, and lidar point cloud data.

- Uncertainties in intents of Google, Amazon, Microsoft, Esri and others to serve standard elevation products, elevation derivatives, and lidar point cloud data to the public as elevation data are provided by Federal agencies or States.

- Uncertainties in elevation data archiving and storage requirements, including funding.

- Uncertainties in the role of "cloud computing."

- Potential risks to the stable funding for elevation data lifecycle acquisition, management and maintenance.

- Changing user requirements or benefits.

A Conceptual Model for the Next-Generation NED 2.0 / 3DEP

With the preceding information in mind, this effort developed some testable methodologies that while they are not exhaustive, they are comprehensive enough to enable NED 2.0 / 3DEP for pseudo implementation. One cautions that there is still a high level of risk involved in this prototype. This prototype had already been tested at the single user level with success; the goal here was to walk that single-user implementation through the full-fledged enterprise operation that spans multiple workflows and ideas of what was the best possible schema. We were not able to test this prototype at the enterprise level. The following was the proposed step-by step process of the lifecycle of a single project through the theoretical NED 2.0 / 3DEP structure. In theory, this should have been a mock exercise that moves a project from receipt to producing NED 2.0 / 3DEP derivative layers and its associated packaging files.

The underlying vision of this direction for NED 2.0 / 3DEP was not to provide static products as the key component, but to develop services that created these standard products and other customizable products. This way a service could have been applied to any data that met defined requirements, either current NED, IFSAR or lidar point cloud data. Rules in these services would have determined what products could have been created from the NED 2.0 / 3DEP source data. Enhanced spatial metadata would have allowed the service to know if the source data met the rules requirements to create the informational derivative product, and what variables the source data could have supported in generating a customized derivative. These services would have been applied in the standard project generation lifecycle and derived results stored in the NED 2.0 / 3DEP backbone or the services would have been called by a web interface to create derived products on the fly. The trade-off between storage space and processing speed will need to be analyzed, and will vary on the derived product (fig. 3).

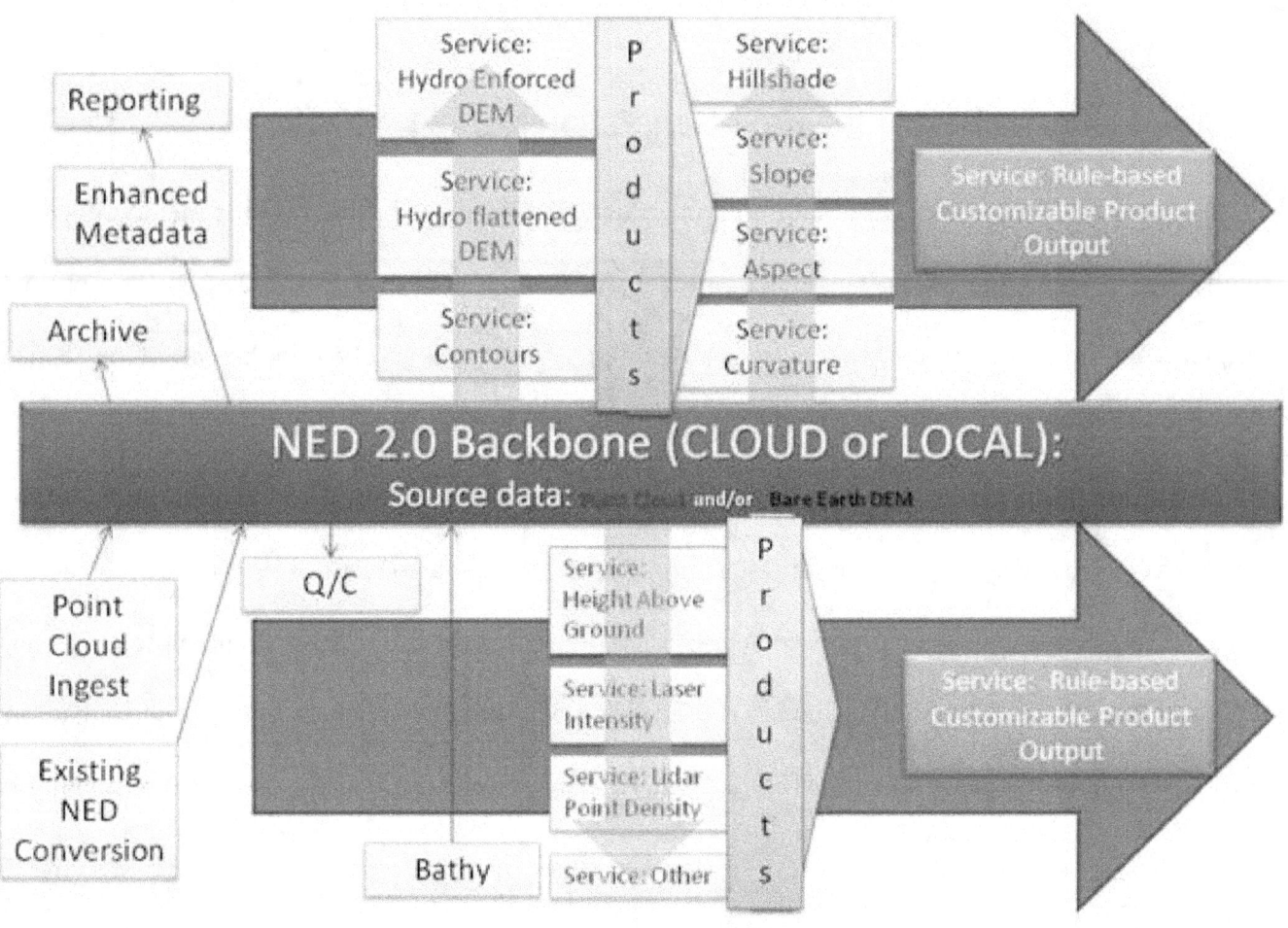

Figure 3.   The proposed framework for the new National Elevation Dataset (red text = lidar only).

The source data could have been stored in the NED 2.0 / 3DEP backbone—this could have been a single location or a pointer to distributed data or data in a cloud. Service nodes would have been connected to the backbone that creates the derived products. The attributes in the enhanced metadata theoretically determined if the source data supported creating those derivatives or not, based on pre-defined rules, such as: one cannot create a height above ground product if the only data available in that area are a bare-earth DEM. One could not create a lidar intensity image if there were not lidar data in that area. We could have then generated derived products from the data in the backbone, or simply called the derived data in the backbone if they were available for a standard product. Another service on the output would have allowed the user to define output variables of each service-derived product. This output service would have been where the data would be converted to file format A, at resolution X in projection Y. If multiple services were called for, this was where the user would have had the option of generating the multiband stack, and determined which derived product they would have wanted in which band. Having services connected to the backbone would in theory allow for an infinite number of services for applications to create an infinite number of products based merely on different or new and improved algorithms. These services could be pre-computed and results stored or called on the fly by web interface and delivered in near real time. The key to determining this would be a cost/benefit assessment of pre-computing these derived layers compared to creating derivatives on the fly. For example, it makes no sense to create a 1-meter DEM for the entire United States and store it statically if only a fraction of the country needs that level of detail. In essence this would be an exercise of determining cost/benefits of storage compared to processing power and speed. Recording popularity of areas of interest, services, and their associated preferred variables will allow these trade-offs to be refined in the future, optimizing the efficiency of output delivery.

The Mock Development Cycle

The following describes a schedule and discussion of a step-by-step procedure for the mock development. Although the steps have not been completely defined on how they could be accomplished, this workflow included some basic data management procedures.

- **Ingestion**

  - Data need to be transmitted by the data source to the entity responsible for managing these data in the context of the national program. Depending on the direction of the program, these data sources could be data collection contractors or other local, State, or Federal government agencies. The size of the data generally dictate delivery of the data on a removable media drive, but options for online delivery might be viable as well. These data could be transferred to a machine owned by the managing entity to be used later in the workflow.

- **Quality Control**

  - Some level of assessment would be needed to determine if the incoming data are suitable for integration into the larger national data repository. However, the key difference in this step compared to the current processes is the fact that the quality control process is performed on the source data, which usually would be the classified point clouds. This assessment would vary based on the program requirements, but can include an independent review of data collection contractor deliverables to ensure that the data meet contracted specifications, or alternatively a less complete review to ensure that the deliverable was formatted appropriately for integration, with duties of full quality control left to another entity.

  - In support of quality control efforts, automated quality checks might be performed to review the data for suitability for integration into the national repository. These automated checks would vary based on the data requirements of the program, but should include a review of the projection of the data, metadata, statistics on data point positions and values, and so on. Automated quality checks should never replace manual checks; however, there are certain functions that would be best automated. For example, checking that the .las files were fully populated, the metadata met specification, the data had no gaps, and so on, could be automated, allowing time for manual checking of non-standardized events. This automation could be outsourced or contracted by a software vehicle to allow for more USGS labor resources to be devoted for certification, manual editing and retraining.

- Create data documentation. Processing could be performed to automatically review the data and compile information about the data, including spatial extent, point density, number of points, spatial reference, and so on, that could be integrated into metadata or other data documentation. A new metadata template and spatial metadata process would need to be developed to provide the correct information to the customer in an easy, intuitive, and informative manner. Research on best practices and methodology need to be encouraged.

- **Data Archive**
  - Once the data have been deemed suitable for integration, the source data must be archived into a formal repository housing enhanced elevation for the Nation. This archive should contain at least two copies in two physically distinct locations that allow for redundancy in situations where one copy becomes unusable. Depending on the program requirements, this archive may include the original data received from the source provider, the data modified as part of the data processing task (below), or both.

- **Data Processing**

  - The key to the success of this conceptual model would be the incorporation and standardization of the incoming data into the backbone. Some processing of data may be needed to reformat the source data for integration into the national repository or to create derivative products. The amount of processing might be affected by the consistency of data coming from source providers, which might be directed by standards set forth from the national program. In addition, the amount of processing needed would also be affected by the products that are developed as part of the national program (such as DEMs, contours, etc.), which would require processing to transform the source data into these products.

  - Ideally, all of the data in the future would be collected to the same standards, so integration of disparate data into a single database would be easier than it currently is. Differences in resolution, projection, vertical and horizontal units, collection timing, and even systems in current data make integrating overlapping lidar datasets difficult to do. An option for NED 2.0 / 3DEP would be to preprocess all disparate data to some kind of consistent, systematic format, and provide spatial metadata to the user to warn them that the derived informational products had been computed using reprocessed, standardized source data. If that reprocessed, standardized source data had not been certified by USGS QC procedures, but the source data had been certified, the user could have the option to run a custom solution using the original source. Cost/benefits and methods of reprocessing existing data should be a topic of active research and operations, if NED is to utilize any existing lidar data.

- **Create Derivative Products**

  - For NED 2.0 / 3DEP, the point cloud data would be where most of the source data from which all derived products are subsequently produced.

  - There is no reason for the NED 2.0 / 3DEP to stop producing what it currently produces. The 1-1/3rd, and 1/9th arc-second data are still extremely valuable and bare-earth DEMs are the primary derivative of lidar today. The changes would be enhancements to the current process. The documented desire for the USGS to produce 1/27th arc second bare-earth elevation data cannot be simply added to the current process because of the way the data are currently organized, but must rely on a new process to function properly.

  - The types of derivative layers to be produced have been documented above. The creation of these derivative products should consist of USGS approved, authoritative routines and input values for those routines, as well as the option for the user to 'turn the knobs' on these values to create a customized product that may better suit their needs, within the appropriateness of the source data to do so. For example, the USGS would have an accepted routine (and probably pre-compute routine) to create 3-meter DEMs; however, if the source data supported 1-meter DEMs, the user could 'turn the knob' to have a service routine generate a 1-meter DEM for their area of interest. Predefined rules would not allow the user to create derivatives that the USGS deemed the data did not support.

  - There are a couple of options for calling routines instead of precomputing layers. First, a web-based interface where the user would select data and an area, provide input for the program for what they want to compute and how they would like the information product back. This option is the model OpenTopography and Digital Coast use. Second, being able to call processing routines from COTS software on NED 2.0 / 3DEP data could be performed via command calls through a web interface.

- The derivative products should always begin from the same, certified source data if possible to ensure consistent results. If the same algorithm runs on the same data, the same results would be expected. The USGS would want to certify the source data, but not necessarily the reprocessed, normalized data, without proper QA/QC on the reprocessed data.

- The USGS would certify an approved, accepted algorithm or model that is being performed on the data. The user would have the option to use that algorithm and variables to generate informational products that the USGS has proven to be successful, as well as have the option to adjust the parameters to that model to best meet user requirements if needed. The USGS would not certify the derived products from any algorithms that may deviate from the USGS 'standard', and this information would be contained in the metadata.

- For derivative products that the USGS deemed popular, staff would most likely pre-compute these layers and store them for download instead of recomputing the same layers repeatedly. What layers would be pre-computed would depend on the following:

    1. Storage needed;

    2. Popularity; and,

    3. Data currency.

- Smaller-sized files, such as the 1- and 1/3rd-arc second DEMs and hillshades should probably be precomputed (as they are now), as the products require minimal storage and are still quite popular. Computer-intensive, high resolution derivative products would most likely not be precomputed with the authoritative routines, but would be generated on an as-needed basis. The system should record in spatial metadata the number of requests per derivative layer with associated variable option selections, and if that number of requests reaches a certain threshold, then that product would most likely be stored in cache for quicker information product delivery. This method could be constantly adjusted for flexible storage needs, which is relevant for assessing cloud computing resource costs

- In the case of multitemporal or overlapping data, precomputing the 'best available' data would continue; however, if older data did exist, there could be the opportunity to generate a customized derived information product from these older data. If every source dataset had been approved for that time frame and the algorithm to generate informational products had been approved, it is assumed that these products would be viable, no matter which one was used. However, the USGS could not guarantee seamlessness, as actual topographic change could create differing products from different time periods (e.g., different water levels or snowpack between collections).

- Any incorporation of multitemporal or multiproject data by an algorithm to generate a derivative would carry that information and associated caveats in the metadata. All of this would be automated by a rule-based metadata generation tool that queried the source data and the algorithm before it wrote the metadata file and associated spatial information.

- The assumed most efficient way of creating derivative products is to run processes on the back end and only deliver the desired information product; however, this is a function of the user's bandwidth, expertise, local computing power, and the server load of the NED 2.0 / 3DEP processors. It may be faster for the user to download the data locally and process it locally than wait in a queue for results. Best practices of derivative product generation needs to be an active topic of research.

- Each of these tasks will drive the needs of the technology infrastructure to ensure that the capacity exists to effectively store data, process data, and serve the data to the public.

An Example Using Real Data

The following is an example demonstration of this concept from start to finish using an existing lidar point cloud source dataset. A dataset collected for Grand County, Colorado (Colo.), was used for the example. Assumptions were that the data were classified properly, and all spatial metadata and preprocessed derivative data were approved. In fact, in this example, no preprocessed derivatives were received, so all services were performed on the point clouds. This example is not an exhaustive process description or algorithm; this case is merely to demonstrate proof-of-concept of how this service might be performed. Further research is needed to determine full optimizations, methodology for seamless stitching, overlapping, or multitemporal datasets, and thorough explanation of processing in a cloud environment. The steps below merely describe general processes to creating standardized and customized products from services on the fly.

- **Ingestion**
  - Data for Grand County, Colo., were received from the vendor. Data included 562 .las files, and all data in total were 112 gigabytes in size. Data included spatial metadata and a lidar processing report created by the vendor, with appropriate accuracies and projection information.
  - The 562 .las files were uploaded into the NED 2.0 / 3DEP backbone, which reside in a theoretical cloud. Tracking software informed the QC team that the data were ready for QC, organization and archive.

- **Quality Control**

  - Once the data were in the NED 2.0 / 3DEP backbone in either the cloud or on local servers, QC was performed on the point clouds. No errors were found in the point cloud data (fig. 4.)

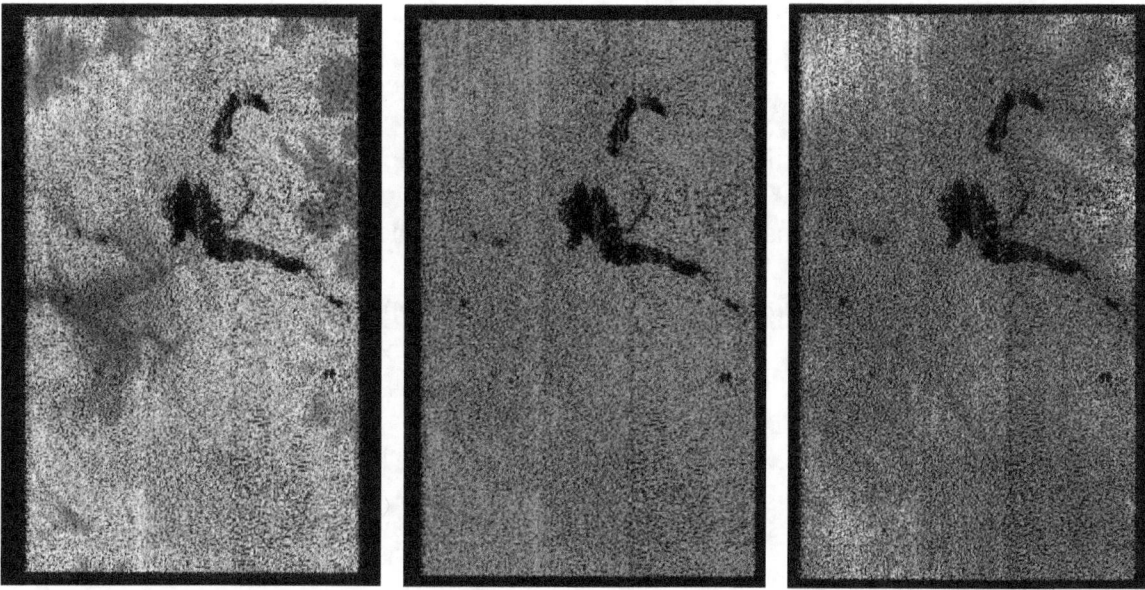

Figure 4.   Quality control of lidar point cloud.

- **Data Archive**

  - Data in the cloud were tagged 'approved' and the National Archives and Records Administration (NARA) archivists were notified that the source data were ready for long-term archiving.

- **Data Processing**

  - The point cloud data were renamed in a catalog convention that allowed all files to have unique identifiers incorporating temporal information, as well as consistent project or location-based naming conventions. The data were then considered in a managed state, and were copied to the partition of the cloud that allowed for direct access to the data. The project boundary and its associated spatial metadata were merged with the existing NED 2.0 / 3DEP database, which was then replicated onto the web server.

- **Create Derivative Products**

  - A web portal allowed the user to run services that produced derivatives from the point cloud data. There were several different services that could be called, depending on the derivative. An invisible index file of all lidar tiles allowed the web application to query which tiles to process. The following examples demonstrate calls to LasTools routines by Martin Isenberg (*http://www.cs.unc.edu/~isenburg/lastools/*) and ArcGIS geoprocessing scripts. There were many different routines that could perform services. The following is a demonstrated proof-of-concept using one method. Keywords in blue were variables that could be manipulated in the customization procedures. These examples worked on this entire project; however, an additional tile picking or clipping service could have been used for subsets of the project. Several services could be strung together in a processing chain. For example, to obtain aspect, one must first calculate a DEM/DSM, and then run the aspect service. For this dataset, the services that are demonstrated were as follows:

- **Export Point Cloud** (fig. 5);

  - lasmerge -lof file_list.txt -o out.laz

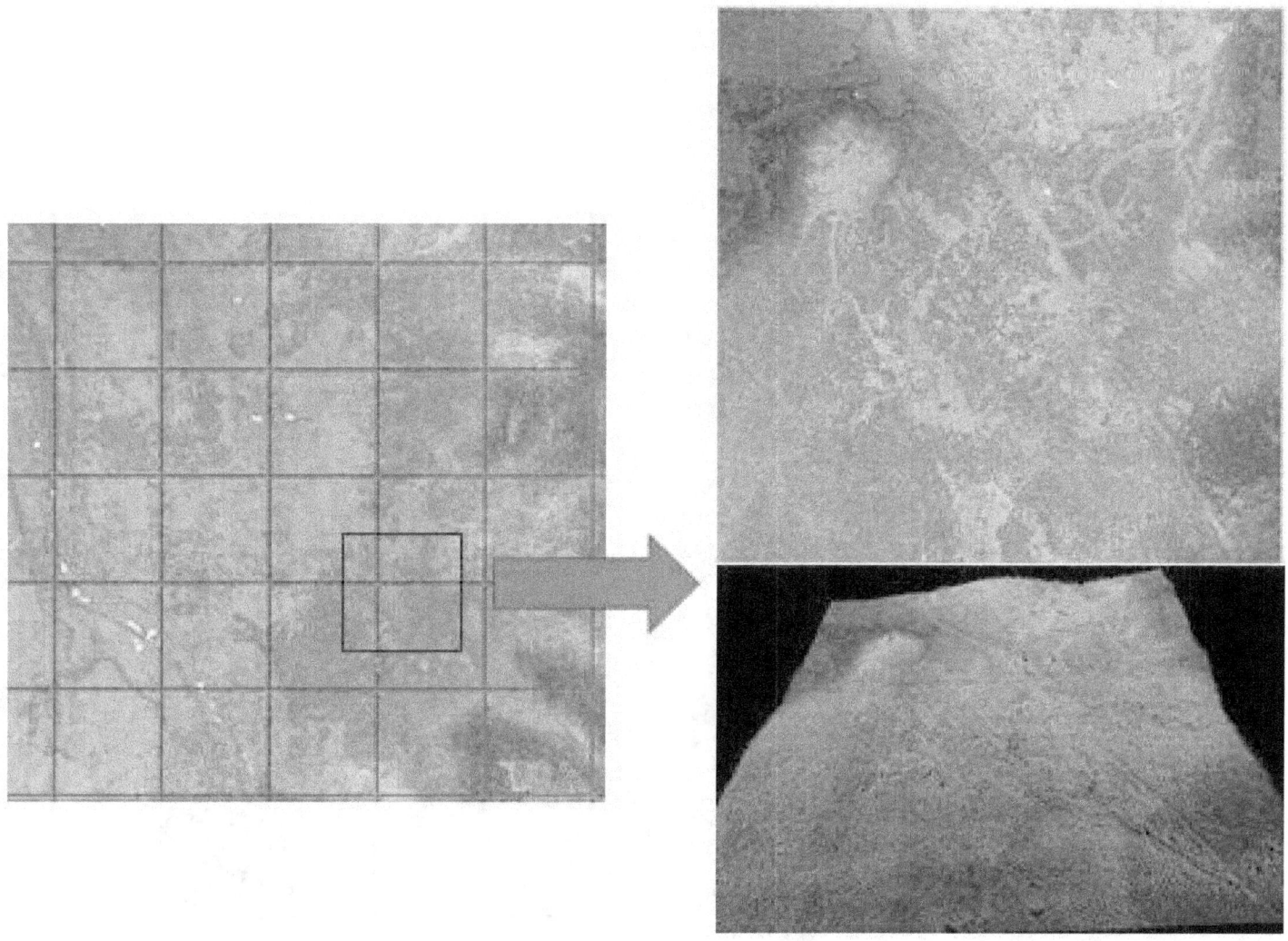

Figure 5. Exporting point clouds.

- **Generate DSM** (fig. 6);

  - blast2dem -lof file_list.txt -o out.tif -step 1

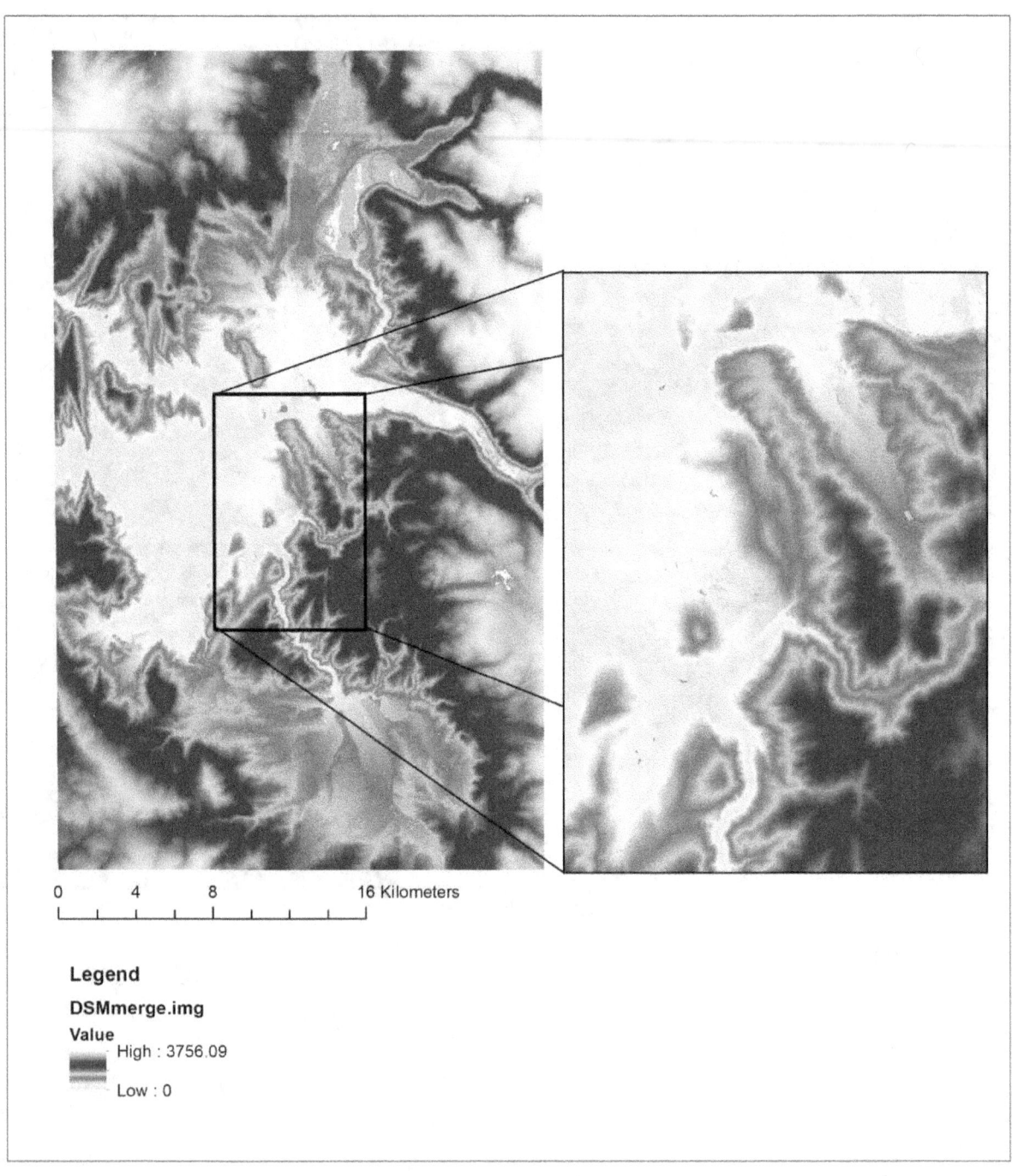

Figure 6.   Generate Digital Surface Model.

- **Generate DTM/DEM** (fig. 7);

    - blast2dem -lof file_list.txt -merged -o dem.img -keep_class 2 -step 1

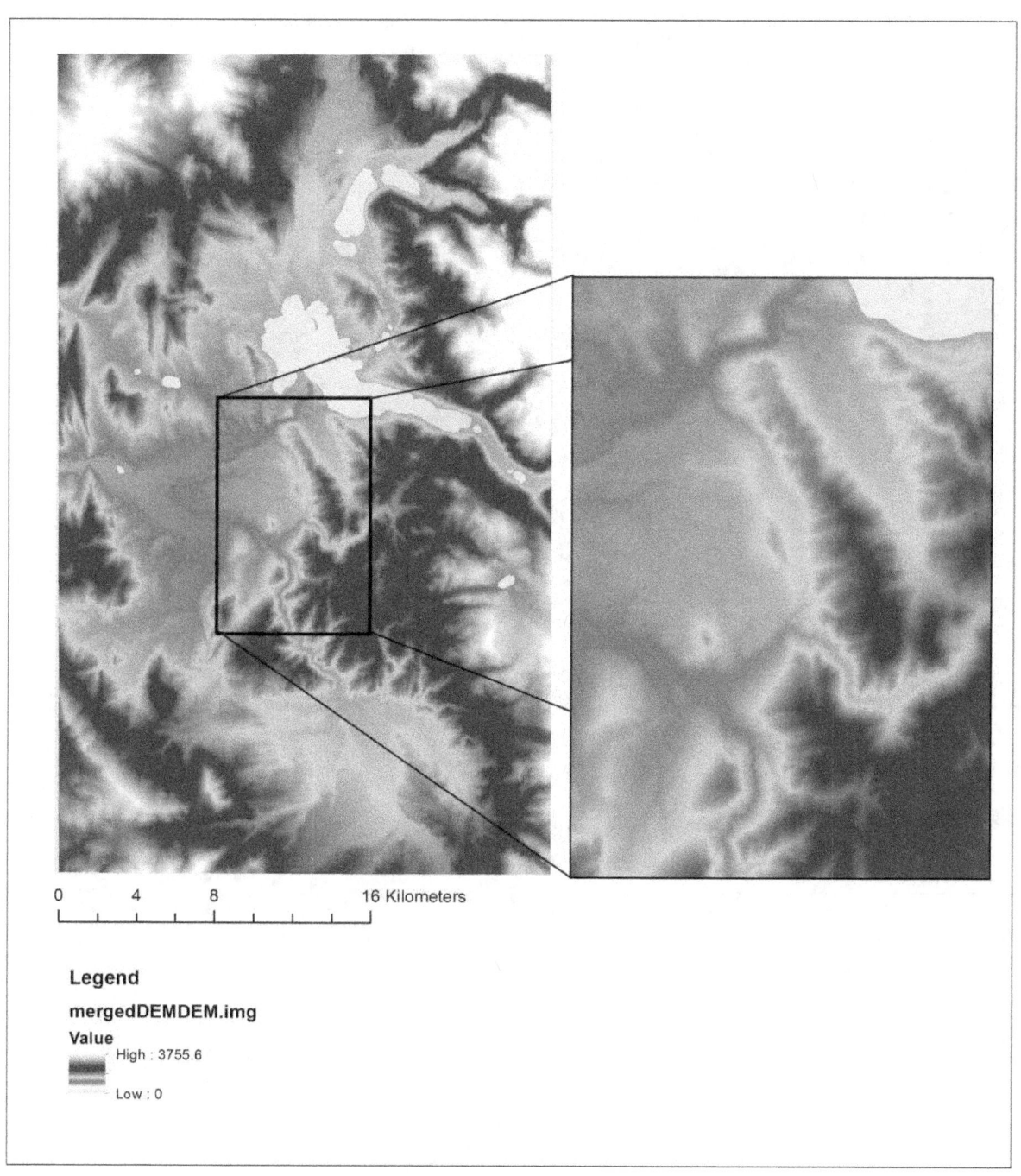

Figure 7.   Generated Digital Elevation Model.

- **Slope** (fig. 8);

  - outSlope = Slope(DEM.img, outMeasurement, zFactor)

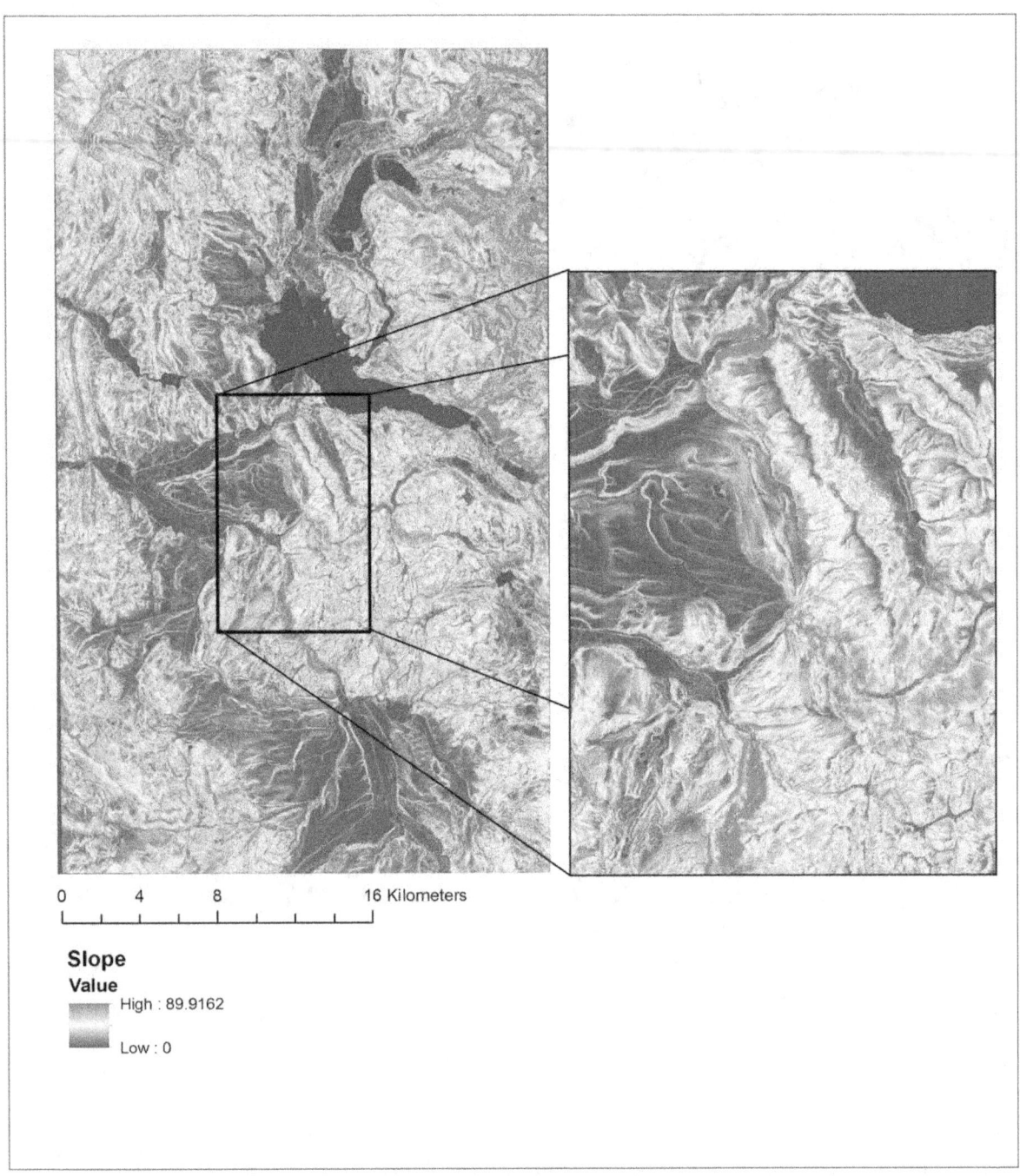

Figure 8. Slope of Digital Elevation Model.

- **Aspect** (fig. 9);

  - outAspect = Aspect(DEM.img)

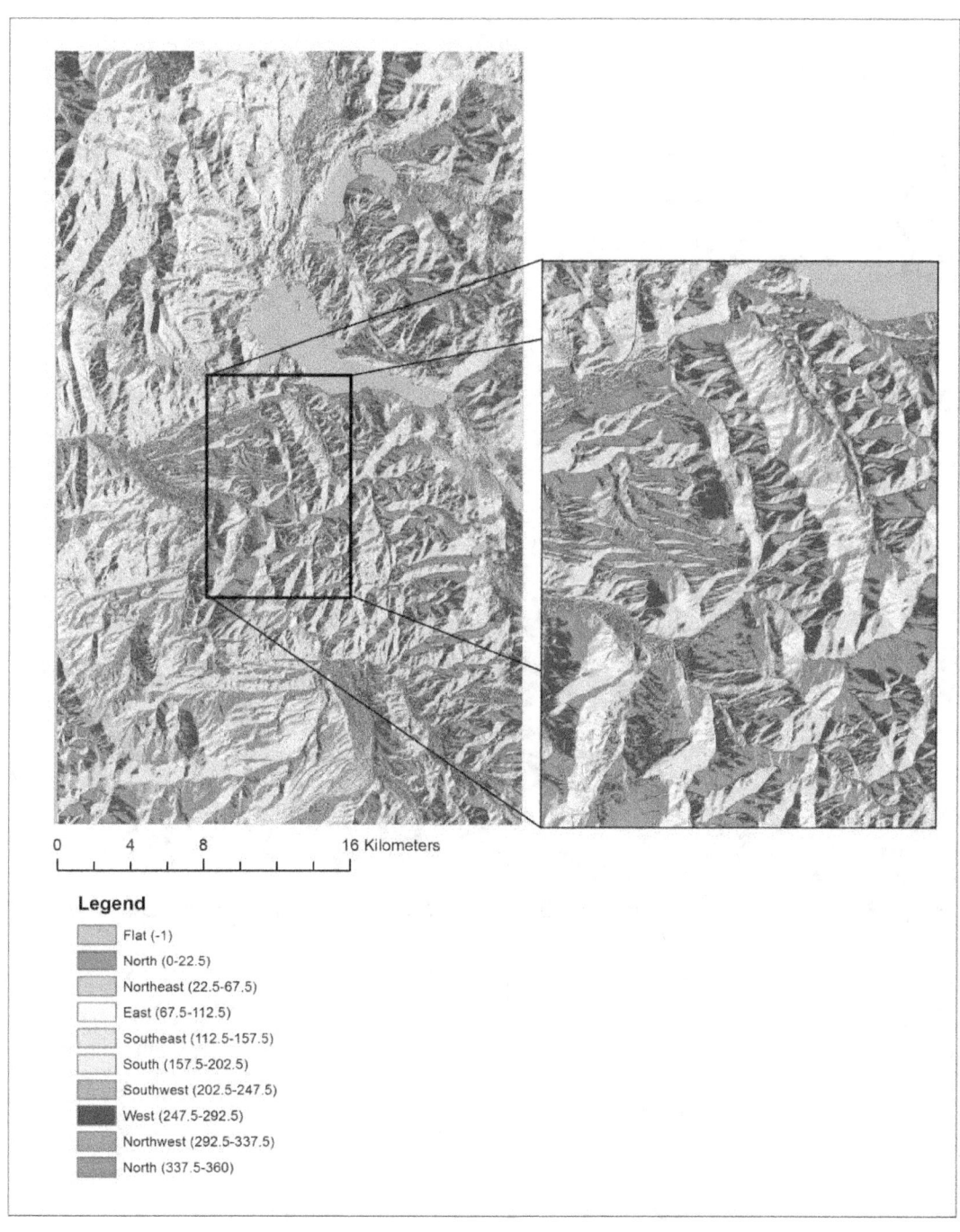

Figure 9. Aspect of Digital Elevation Model.

- **Hillshade** (fig. 10);

  - outHillShade = HillShade(DEM.img, azimuth, altitude, modelShadows, zFactor)

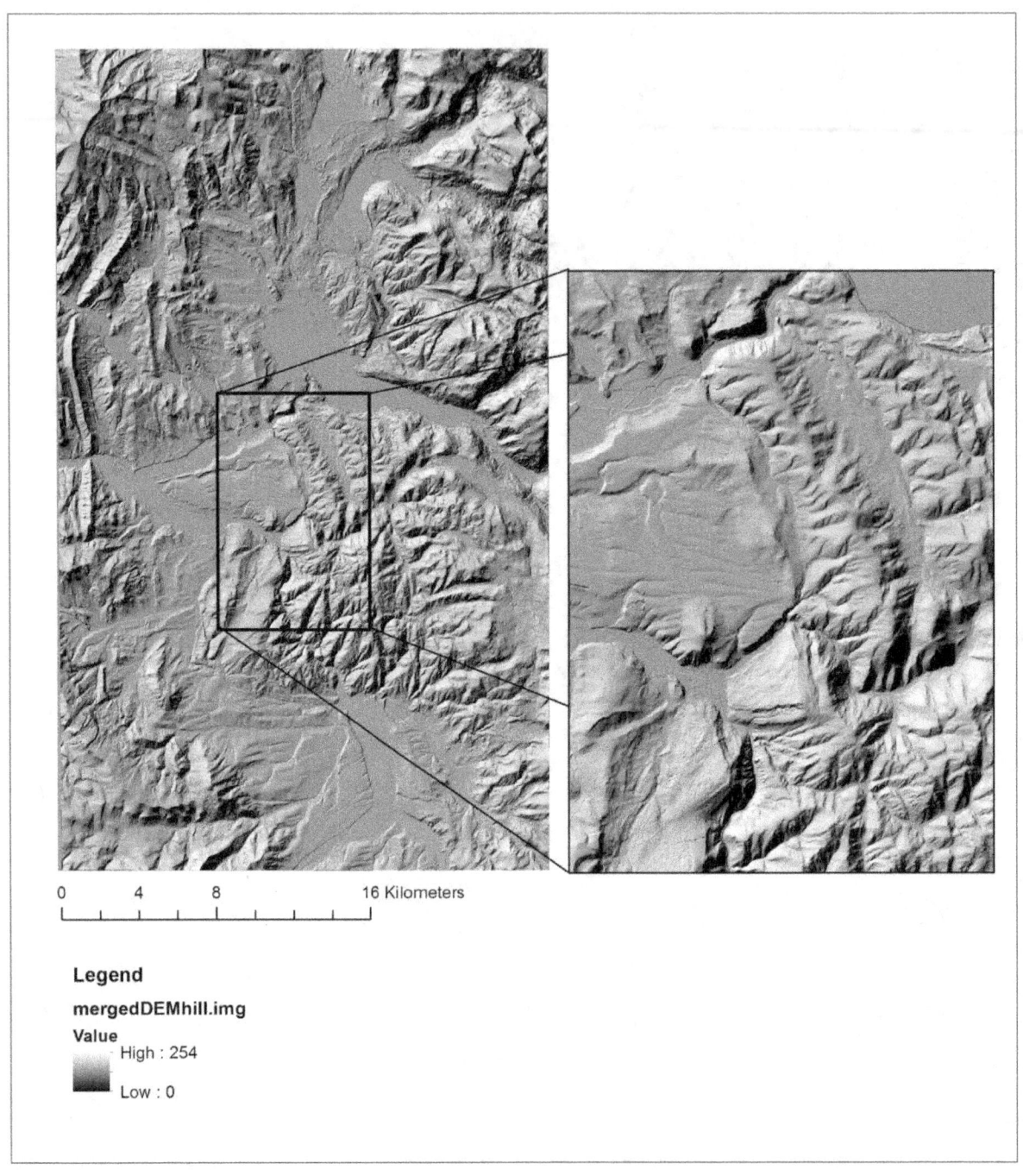

Figure 10.   Hillshade of Digital Elevation Model.

- **Curvature** (fig. 11);

    - outCurve = Curvature(inRaster, 1.094)

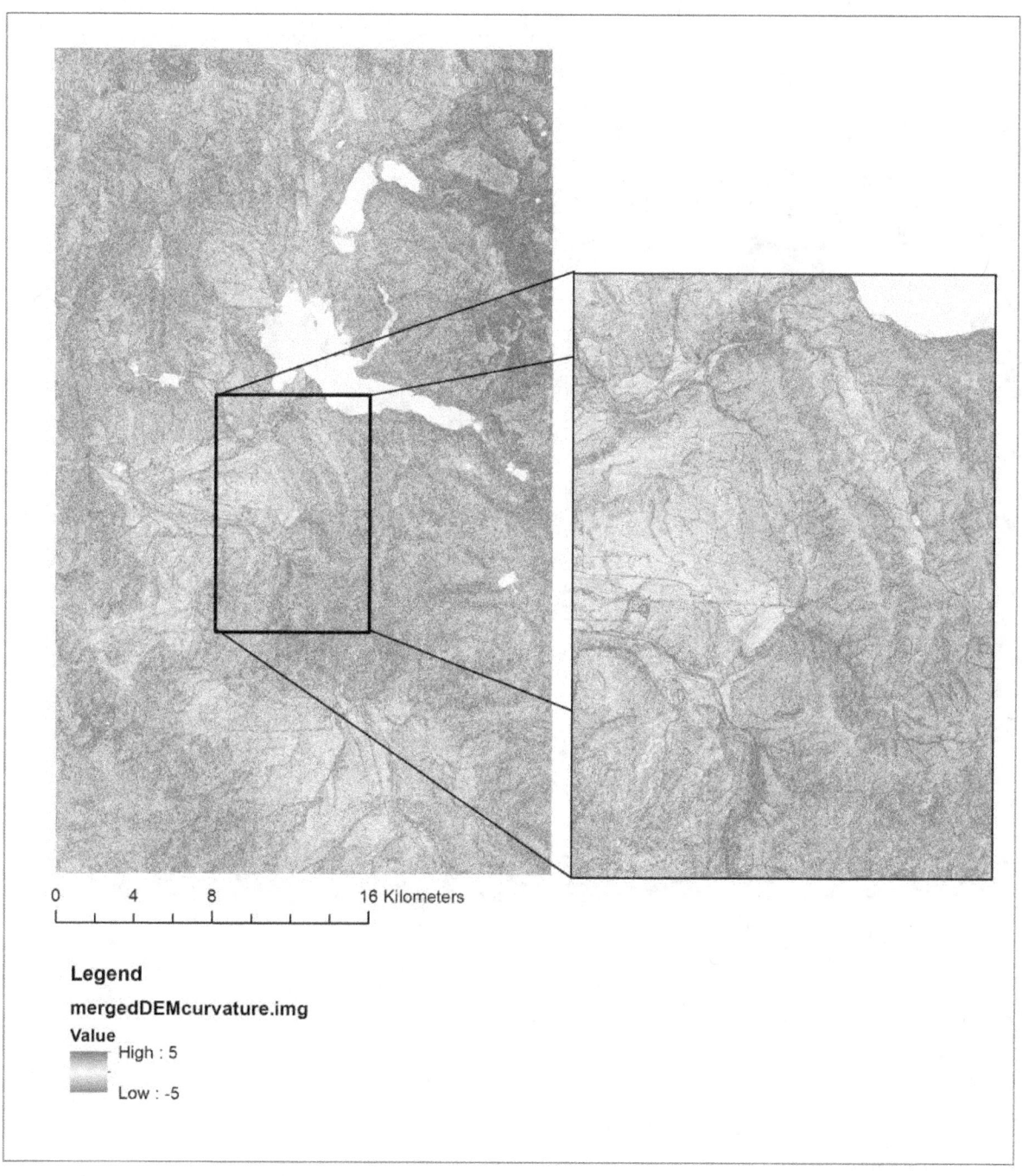

Figure 11. Curvature of Digital Elevation Model.

- **Height Above Ground** (fig. 12);

  - lasheight –lof lidar_files.txt -o out.las -replace_z
  - blast2dem -i out.las –merged -o HAG3m.img -step 3

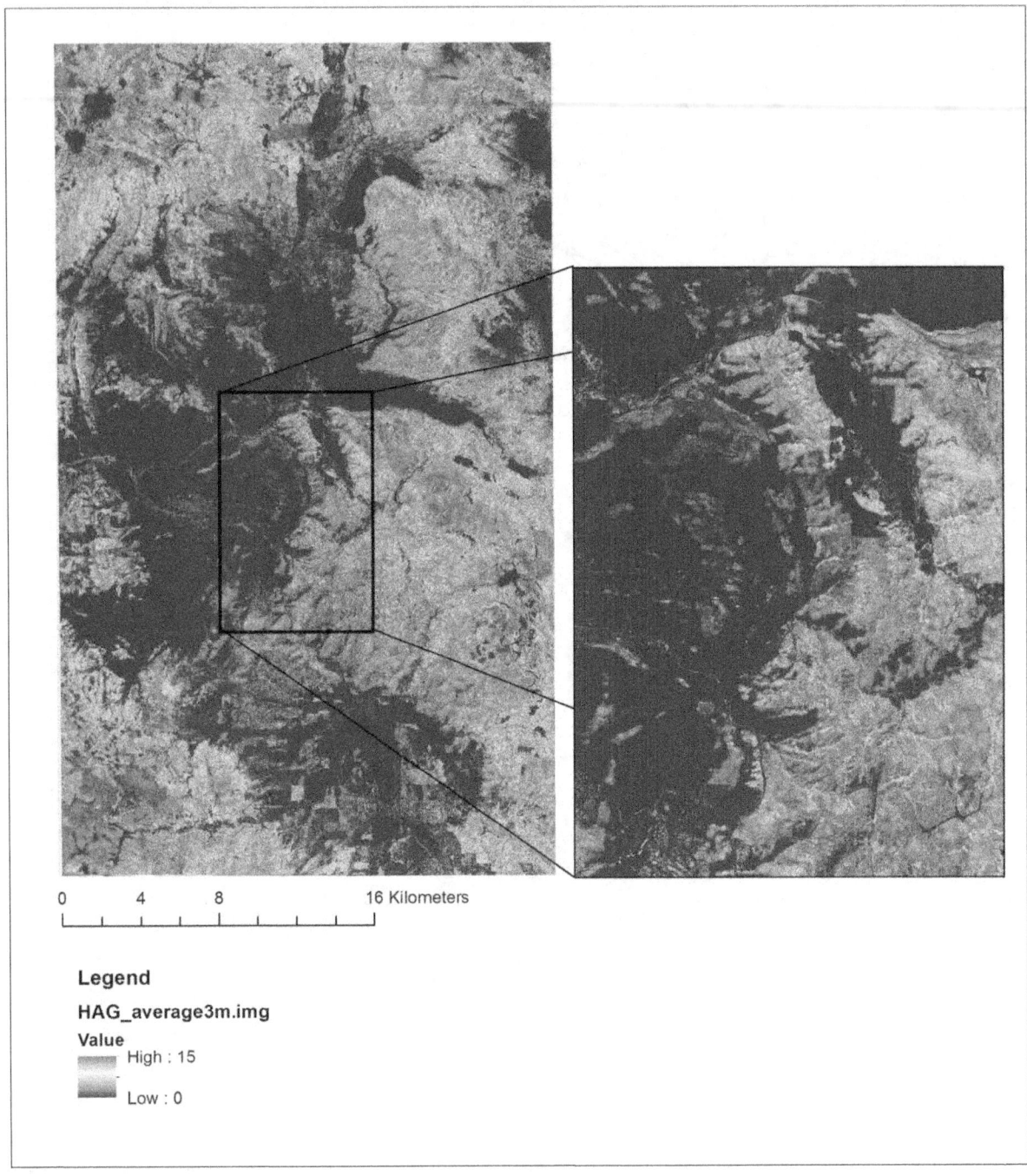

Figure 12. Height above ground.

- **Laser Intensity**

  - lasgrid -v -lof lidar_files.txt –merged –o int.img -step 3

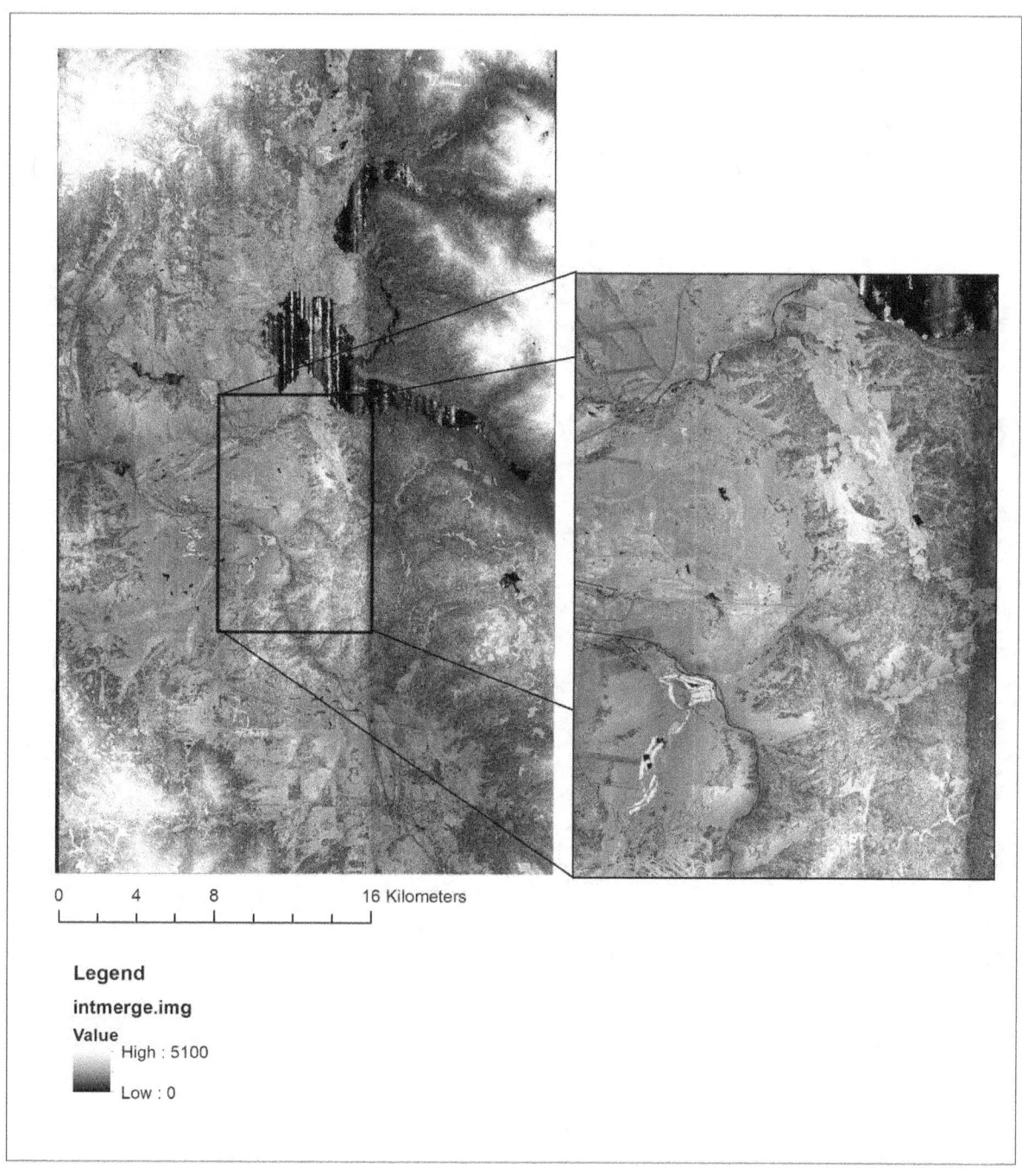

Figure 13. Laser intensity.

- **Point Density**

lasgrid -v -lof lidar_files.txt -o out.bil -density_16bit -step 3

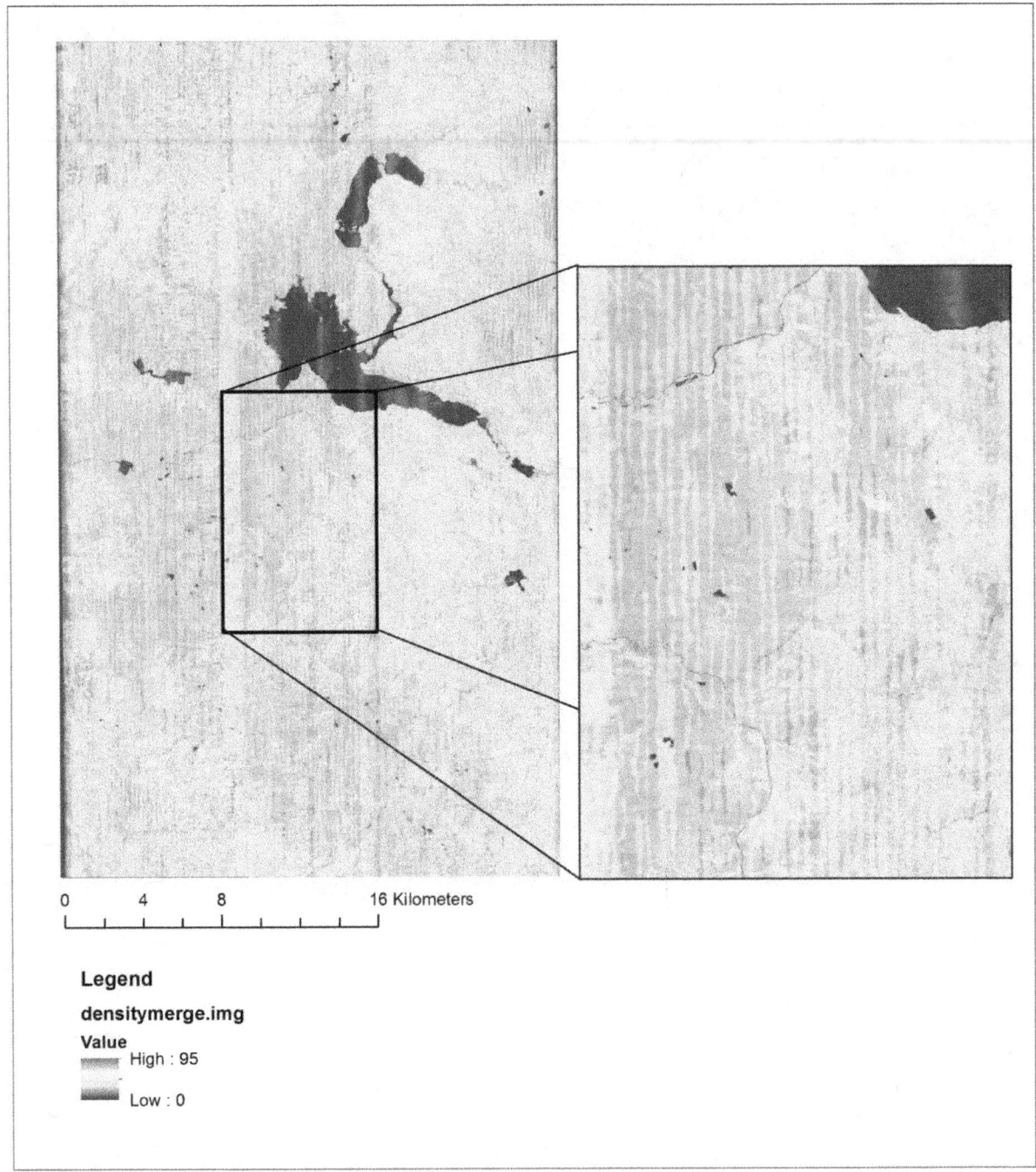

Figure 14. Point density.

- For each of these derivatives, there were several rule-based options to choose from:

    - Resolution (-step x)

        - Not applicable for point cloud, however, one could thin the points. For example, output every nth point.

    - Projection

    - File type/file format

- Many different types of services could be strung together as well. For example, one could create a slope map of the Height Above Ground layer (fig. 15):

  - lasheight -i in.las -o out.las -replace_z

  - blast2dem -i out.las -o HAGout.tif -step 3

  - outSlope = Slope(HAGout.tif, outMeasurement, zFactor)

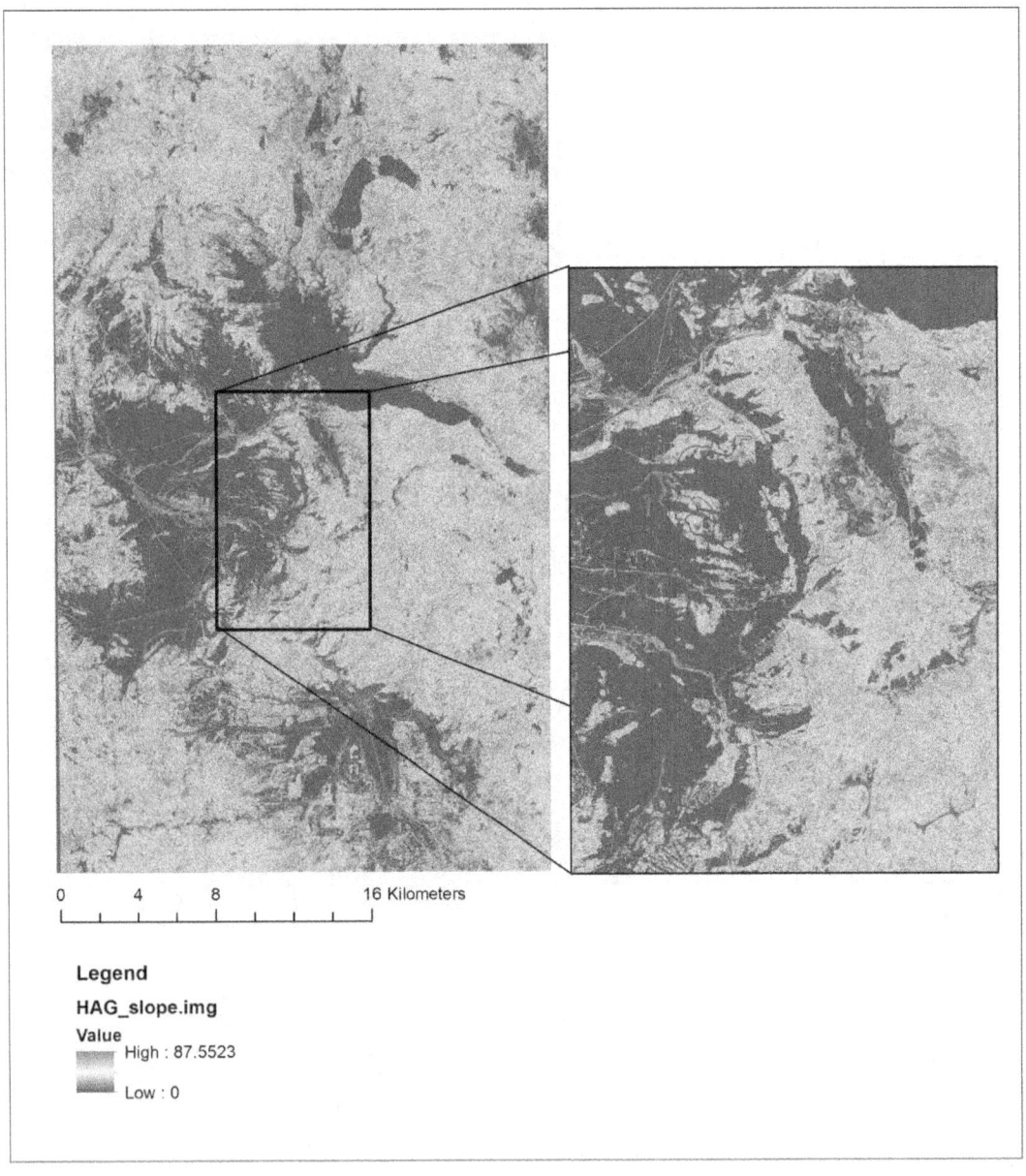

Figure 15.   Slope of the height above ground layer.

- An option was also provided to export several options together into a multiband stack; in several file format options, as described in Stoker (2010) (fig. 16). In this example, Red= HAG slope; Green = HAG; Blue= Laser Intensity;

- CompositeBands_management(outSlope; HAGout.tif; int.img,compbands.tif)

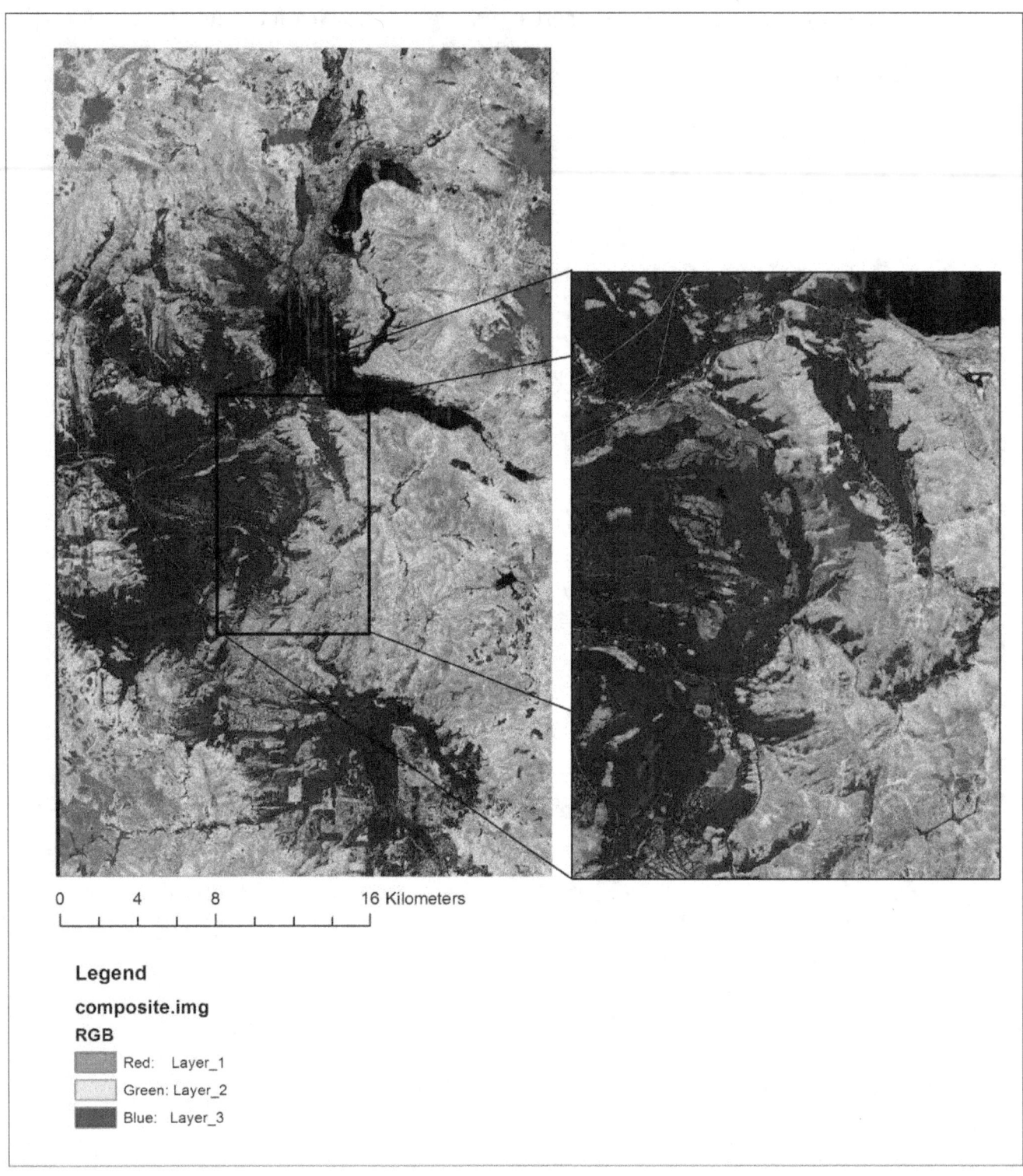

Figure 16. Merging multiple derived layers into a Red/Green/Blue band stack.

Providing a Mechanism for "Plug-Ins"

In the 'big data' environment of 2012, simply providing the access to download the data is no longer enough. Even concepts such as processing on the fly in the mock development cycle will soon be seen as inadequate in the current (2012) geospatial environment. With the development of the cloud and cloud computing (not just cloud storage), methods exist that allow for 3rd party software packages to tap into a data stream and provide customized solutions utilizing the source data. An important goal is to manage all NED 2.0 / 3DEP data in a systematic, consistent way, and publish the source data in a way that other software packages can search, extract, and process those data directly from a cloud environment, potentially opening new markets and new opportunities for the public and private sector to take advantage of the source elevation data. Direct access has advantages as compared to an environment where data are provisioned in bits and pieces or controlled quantities. The real innovations in the future will be enabled when external users have direct access to massive amounts of data all at one time. The USGS may benefit from considering the development of next-generation methods for providing direct access to its archive of 'big data'.

Considerations for Future Work

The USGS is at a potential crossroads when it comes to the future of its mapping programs. The potential exists to completely transform how the agency views, operates, and manages elevation data. The cartographic processes of the past are rapidly giving way to new technologies that directly collect 3D information and place it into a virtual environment capable of the most realistic representations of the Earth possible. The USGS might consider the latest commercial offerings in meeting elevation customer expectations. For the USGS to retain leadership in this field and to be successful in the future, the following actions need to be investigated further:

1. The USGS might consider utilizing new mapping technologies and recruit and retrain lidar/elevation expertise to better support the many activities that would directly benefit from these technologies.

2. While the USGS most likely cannot become a lidar data collection agency, the USGS can retain its leadership in contracting, acquiring, and distributing authoritative data in support of its mapping and science mission. A revamping of quality control procedures that puts primary focus on the point cloud data is needed, and these assessments need to be conducted at the source data level, as well as with the derivatives.

3. A new standardized procedure for acquiring source and derived data needs to be thoroughly researched and adopted to provide means for these disparate datasets to be quickly incorporated together, ideally with minimal manual work needed.

4. A census of prior data that meet or do not meet these new standardization procedures or specification parameters needs to be undertaken. All prior data that meet specifications and standards should be used, whereas all other data should not necessarily be ignored, but be tagged as noncompliant to meet USGS business practices.

5. An adoption of cloud storage and computing protocols needs to be quickly developed, and all data that meet specification should be immediately incorporated into the backbone data structure.

6. The USGS should prioritize development of this backbone structure for the source data; preferably in a cloud computing infrastructure. Only then should full development of derived products be formally pursued outside of a research and development environment.

7. Applications and technology developments need to be adequately supported to keep pace with fast changing elevation collection technologies and associated methods. The USGS cannot rely solely on a single technology (such as discrete-return lidar only), but needs to develop 3D applications requirements that can be met by a suite of technologies.

Conclusions

This report documents a year-long study that researched and attempted to develop a conceptual framework for a system that can efficiently provide three-dimensional (3D) information in ways that meet defined business use requirements as documented in the National Enhanced Elevation Assessment. Although demonstration of proof-of-concept and considerations for future work are described in this report, this study merely scratched the surface as to what questions need to be answered to confidently deliver a prototype that could support a $146 million per year interagency 3D Elevation Program (3DEP). The fundamentals underlying this system appear sound, but to fully scope an effort of 3DEP magnitude, more refined studies are needed. The suggestions, considerations, and examples documented herein are just part of the research needed for the USGS to confidently move forward with an operational 3DEP.

References Cited

Dewberry, 2011, Final Report of the National Enhanced Elevation Assessment: Fairfax, Va., Dewberry, 84 p. plus appendixes (revised 2012), available at http://www.dewberry.com/Consultants/GeospatialMapping/FinalReport-NationalEnhancedElevationAssessment.

Gesch, D.B., Oimoen, M., Greenlee, S.K., Nelson, C.A., Steuck, M., and Tyler, D., 2002, The National Elevation Dataset: Photogrammetric engineering and remote sensing, v. 68, no. 1, p. 5–11.

Gesch, D.B., 2007, The National Elevation Dataset, chap. 4 *of* Maune, D., ed., Digital elevation model technologies and applications—the DEM users manual, (2d ed.): Bethesda, Md., American Society for Photogrammetry and Remote Sensing, p. 99–118.

Heidemann, Hans Karl, 2012, Lidar base specification version 1.0: U.S. Geological Survey Techniques and Methods, book 11, chap. B4, 63 p.

Snyder, G.I., 2012a. National Enhanced Elevation Assessment at a glance: U.S. Geological Survey Fact Sheet 2012–3088, 2 p.(Also available at http://pubs.usgs.gov/fs/2012/3088/.)

Snyder, G.I., 2012b, The 3D Elevation Program--Summary of Program Direction: U.S. Geological Survey Fact Sheet 2012–3089, 2 p. (Also available at http://pubs.usgs.gov/fs/2012/3089/.)

Stoker, J. M., 2010. Making lidar more photogenic: Creating band combinations from lidar information: Photogrammetric Engineering and Remote Sensing v. 76, no. 36., p. 216–220.